VOICELESS LOVE

poems by

Katherine Brueck

Finishing Line Press
Georgetown, Kentucky

VOICELESS LOVE

ACKNOWLEDGMENTS

"Lamb Without Defense," *Christian Poetry Review International*, April 2000
"Heart Like Glass," *Troubadour: Best of Rhyme*, 2001
"Dance with Trolls," *Tucumcari Literary Review*, March/April 2001
"Bright June," "Evening Serenade," "Jewel," *Mount Voices*, Spring 2002
"Harp of Gold," *Parnassus Literary Journal*, Vol. 27, No. 1, Spring 2003
"Like the Lily," *Blue Unicorn*, Vol. XXIX, Number 2, February 2006

Editor: Christen Kincaid

Cover Art: Wikimedia Commons: Barton Creek Rocks Oil on Canvas

Author Photo: Marcy Dugan Photography

Printed in the USA on acid-free paper.
Order online: www.finishinglinepress.com
also available on amazon.com

Author inquiries and mail orders:
Finishing Line Press
P. O. Box 1626
Georgetown, Kentucky 40324
U. S. A.

Table of Contents

THE THEME: *A Love without Voice*
Philomela 1
Star or Mime 2

FRIENDS/LOVERS
Kemosabe 4
Hint of Sun 5
Silhouette 6
Riot in my Heart 7
Heart like Glass 8
Harp of Gold 9

HUSBAND
Love in Shadow 12

CHILDREN
Children Weeping 14
Wounded Soldier 15
Nightmare 16
Like the Lily 17

MOTHER
Devil's Tear 20
Visitation 21
Riddles of the Tomb 22
Bright June 23
Jewel 24
Evening Serenade 25

FATHER
Old King 28
Nothing 29
Glass of Time 30

GOD: THE CRUCIFIED
Dead Lamb Walking 32
Scarecrow 33
Red Leaves 34

The deepest feeling always shows itself in silence.

Marianne Moore

Preface

Like any variety of the written word, the sonnets of *Voiceless Love* were not written in a vacuum. There is a history to be acknowledged. While the sonnet has long been associated with the theme of love, only gradually have treatments of the theme in the sonnet form been freed from the shackles of convention.

I owe to the fourteenth-century Italian sonneteer Francis Petrarch *(Il Canzoniere)*, the first modern poet, the example of an exploration through language of an identity in love beyond the religious identity of a 13th century medieval artist like Dante Alighiere *(La Vita Nuova)*.

Also I would like to acknowledge the encouraging example of sixteenth-century women sonneteers like Louise Labe (French), Gaspara Stampa (Italian) and Lady Mary Wroth (English) for articulating their own voices even at the risk of alienating their readers. All three women reverse the accepted role of the man as active in love and therefore superior and the woman as passive and therefore inferior. For reversing the standard hierarchy created by men sonneteers, their courageous efforts won these women the titles "prostitute"—as in the case of the two former poets—or "slanderer" in the instance of Lady Mary Wroth. /1/

In the typical 16th century sonnet sequence, say Sir Philip Sidney's "Astrophel and Stella," in the footsteps of Dante's Beatrice and Petrarch's Laura, the woman addressed was often idealized for her spiritual and physical beauty even while the poet's own plight as the rejected or invisible lover was lamented. In the section of *Voiceless Love* devoted to unrequited love, the woman actively experiences love while the passive object is male. The whole experience rather than being idealized in any way, however, is treated as a kind of curse, further distancing my own sonnets from Elizabethan exemplars. It is worth noting that the view of love as poison (witness the ten-year war sparked by Helen of Troy and the suicide and death brought about by the impassioned Phaedra) is much closer to ancient Greek treatments rather than to Elizabethan uses of the sonnet sequence with its idealizing tendencies (FRIENDS/LOVERS: "Dance with Trolls," "Heart Like Glass").

"Love in Shadow, " the one sonnet addressed to my husband, comes closest to idealization of all twenty-five poems in the sequence (HUSBAND) . This sonnet describes what I believe is the best that life has to offer in the way of love—a love between equals that is lasting. But here, countering the conventional impulse to idealize, I emphasize how even an egalitarian married love slides down the "dark tunnel" that awaits all mortal things. The lack of rosy glow in this as in all the poems in the collection I attribute to my view of immortality which I share with the twentieth century French religious philosopher and mystic, Simone Weil. Weil asserts that it is not the business of the human being to think about another world; it is our business to think about this one (see my *The Redemption of Tragedy,* SUNY Press, 1995). The result is that all poems in this sonnet sequence are viewed from the perspective of this world—even those dedicated to love of God which, following a theology of the cross, takes for subject Christ's crucifixion apart from the resurrection (GOD: THE CRUCIFIED—"Dead Lamb Walking," "Red Leaves," "Scarecrow").

Continuing in what is essentially a naturalistic vein, my sonnets on children (CHILDREN) deal with children in terms of unpleasant subjects like parental infidelity ("Children Weeping"), abortion ("Wounded Soldier") and the occasional nightmare experience that can accompany legally raising a child not one's own biologically ("Nightmare"). My treatments of love of mother and father (MOTHER and FATHER) focus on off putting subjects like an incident of molestation ("Nothing") and the irrevocability of personal loss through death ("Jewel"). Thus while taking the subjects which middle class Victorian society recommended for women sonneteers—children, family, religion—I do not treat them, any more than I do unrequited love, in a traditional manner.

Thus the landscape of the present work produces a melancholy for which I believe the song of the nightingale is an appropriate symbol. "Philomela" (THE THEME: A Love without Voice) references the mutilated, mute woman who was metamorphosed into the bird whose beautiful song is distinctive for its sadness.

Any beauty that these sonnets exhibit comes from true and powerful feeling that is at the same time restrained—a formula for poetic beauty as old as the tragedies of ancient Greece. The check on the profoundest emotion which, as the epigraph states always shows itself in silence, is provided throughout by the Elizabethan sonnet form. For help with the difficult issue of emotional restraint in love, ironically, I adhere as closely as possible to what is arguably the most traditional form available to the contemporary poet while remaining unconventional in my treatment of the theme itself.

I would like to acknowledge Holy Trinity Episcopal Church in Westchester CA who by inviting me to present these poems in an in-house speaker series—well before the publication date—gave me occasion to work out the meditation on the sonnet sequence through which this preface came into being.

Katherine Brueck
El Segundo, California

/1/ Ramsden, Catherine Anne, "Desire and Agency in the Modern Woman's Sonnet" (2012). Dissertation. Paper 541. http://ecommons. edu/luc_diss/541

The THEME: A Love without Voice

Philomela

Pretty bird, broken-winged, lies voiceless beneath
Pale sky, feather dropping blue
On leaves of grass. Ancient petal, wreath
Of browning weed, enshrouding bright dew,
Chilling hemlock, insidiously seep
Into naked flesh, weep in tune
To barren earth: day forgotten, leap
Beyond dark bridge, man crucified at noon
For voiceless love. Like Philomela,
Mouthing moan in darkness, I cry nor wail,
Red tongue cut at root, word beyond chill
Grave or warmth of womb: no nightingale
Of soul's window or flash beyond lambent
Eye or living letter of kisses sent.

Star or Mime

Pure as mercury love goes down:
Kills or cures heart of cannibal.
Silence cuts bold slice of antic noun
Posing as tempestuous verb: fine jewel.
Wordlessness speaks at quiet times,
Insinuating space between odd blocks,
Strutting on broad stage, star or mime,
Shouting golden words enviers mock.
A solitude, soft presence speaks, stutters
Profound feeling, inexpressible.
Falling snowflakes earthward slowly mutter
Enchanting words spoken in full lull.
Feather falls, dances through fine air
As quietness whispers secret care.

FRIENDS/LOVERS

Kemosabe

You find me, legs motionless: redbound at noon,
Raise me, voiceless, with demanding love.
You bend my limbs, crunch bones until soon
I moan wingless in new shroud of black dove.
Only meat of wholeness will satisfy,
Leg fashioned of newborn flesh, slowly, for me:
Two oiled hands wandering my thigh.
Locked shoulders, closed back, I seek birthing key.
As suns rise and sink, no respite, you tend me,
Teach me to rise and walk again, to view
Blank world through brightening glass, freed
Of despair, of desiccation through dew.
Kemosabe, magician, faithful friend—
You brandish wand of healing as I attend.

Hint of Sun

Deep down, a still small voice is calling me,
Crying to be born, impossible.
A something in the sky yearns to be,
Though grey clouds, forthright, amass until
Hint of sun slips toward sea and sand,
Glimmers as it flickers once or twice,
Dims, washes away from sea to land.
Echoes of the past, drowning, voice
Melodies scarcely heard. Tunes alive,
Though dying, sound minor chord: music
In black night. Candlelight revives
A singing sound of burning in the wick.
If time had been kinder, in its cruel way,
Flames of love would torch the light of day.

Silhouette

Shadow falls across stark bed at dawn
As eyes open, groggy from dream of you.
Arms embrace nearness though feel you gone,
Hope to hold a face or hand, in lieu
Of darkness just caressing silken sheet.
Linen washes once more—your absence sullies
Silhouette of you. Telltale wind meets
Breath as gust blows bent body to knees,
Weak with fine-spun prayer: idolatry.
Your eyes appear: invisible woven threads
Shape darkness or light, joy or misery
As I crochet blank heart alive or dead.
Forever you enter, exit amber room
As hopeful fingers weave sunlight on the loom.

Riot in my Heart

Dark glasses dangled—the day your eyes fixed mine,
Shining blue, burning childlike flesh
With unsought rays of light, grilling fine
Pink heart until riven in two, or fresh
Skin until you scorched, branded me
With weapons of merry talk, lively grace.
Armor, relentless, hung for all to see
In closet, evening of your embrace,
Hour of riot in my heart, still not
Quelled: months later no police have come,
Bringing peace or rest, but your lips caught
Fleeing tongue, straying impassioned, hummed
Littering tunes of love. Reason, sleeping,
Holds aloof as I stand naked: weeping

Heart like Glass

Like broken glass, my heart jags skin all day,
Sadly picks up the nerve, presses the vein.
The blood pumps outrageously: I lay
My raised hopes down; I forfeit all dreams, as pain
Sings in whispers to the trumpets of time.
Longing lifts my bones, stretches my sides
Until I see joy from afar: a mirage or a mime.
When I walk I bruise, when I stride
I stumble. I fall in the dust of my love, never fed.
I seek a pill, a potion, an elixir, a cure:
I reach for a hand, a face, a hair of the head.
I grab the air: nothing, no one—too pure.
When will the eery path disappear? When will I
Awaken, spell gone, eager to live—then to die?

Harp of Gold

Shining girl, I darken all the stairs,
Sigh as shirtless men race or fly:
Through glasses I see your baby face, hairs
Askew, smiling to yourself as my
Snaps, sashes, buttons come undone.
You jog past me, flitting on every other
Step, sullying my sleeves. The sun
Abruptly vanishes: red ribbons mother
Tied loosen, fade to your indifferent stride.
A lonely harp sounds inside my breast,
Shakes with rhythm unfulfilled: bride
Of brokenness, golden, welcome guest
To nothingness or vacuous pain. I cover
Face, forsaken: homing pigeons hover.

HUSBAND

Love in Shadow

Shadows seem to wave their hands to me:
You, dignified, undulate in mist
As the bright day parades in green. I see
Gray flowers through a lattice hang and twist
And blow in silver silence around your form.
The sun reflects your figure upon the wall:
I have caressed your body, sweet and warm.
Down a dark tunnel, I'll embrace cold flesh, call
In vain to a shape without a soul. How will eyes,
In jagged pieces, see again? How remember
Touch of living hands? I'll ask why
You and I could not to every September
Have sung or wildly whispered the greeting
Of our constant love: a shadow meeting.

CHILDREN

Children Weeping

Wind lulls approaching sound of children weeping:
I lie awake, lover in my arms.
Chant of sorrow slowly creeping
Through cold night never fully harms
Me, strong in adulthood, bound round by my
New love. Eerie broken wails tap
Bolted door, scratch frosted window, pry
Fresh sheets of close embrace, rudely lap
Drops of sweat, tweak languishing breast.
Cries of children echo in the dark,
Probe heart, invincible, dressed
In robes, radiant with ruby stones. Lark
Of passion drowns voiceless haunting sound
Of children weeping, lost, though I am found

Wounded Soldier

Child of love plays in house of glass,
Green eye blue with sorrow. Great with grief:
Something sad or sacred pushes—last
Labor, first. Paradise grows leaf
Of misery: ancient toy chest opens,
Vacant in misty corner, hollow sound
Echoes as lid of childhood shuts. Your friends
Try; but only you carry pound-
Of-flesh-to-be, invaded darling, wounded soldier
In woman's war of love, musket cracked,
Cast aside, indifferent, grief pining in your
Arm, wailing without voice, rack
Of words gone wrong. Divine Mother's mark
Shines like foil over child-woman in darkness.

Nightmare

Sometimes I stop to watch while you are sleeping,
My daughter, my love—nine and a half years of age.
A busy day done, shopping, skating can bring
Sweet dreams, soft rest; or sometimes feelings of rage
Will creep at night into your pillow and plague
You too with nightmare: you talk, you scream aloud.
Sometimes I dream I've lost you to horrors vague,
Or a phantom arises, from earth by a stranger ploughed:
Your birthmother appears and smiles; she embraces you.
You gaze at her, give her loving kiss.
Together you walk away, forgetting who
Watches from inside—a woman who'll miss
Her daughter, her only child. I stare from afar:
I wait an eternity, my door ajar.

Like the Lily

Flight of those sweet birds, the years, disallows
My knowing you or loving you as people
Do glass seas or diamonds. You grow
Like the lily, neither push nor pull,
Toil nor spin. You are arrayed
Like one, my calf of burnished gold, earth's promised queen.
As a colt you whinnied, bucked, obeyed;
A pygmy student, laughing (gay or mean),
You graced the day you rose into, glad morn
On which I, adoring subject, bowed
The loving knee. Now your green eyes, forlorn,
Seek a sun I no longer see. Proud,
You step out into a bright new world
I too once wandered, blinded: shining pearl.

MOTHER

Devil's Tear

She lays herself down—leaden winter day—
Readies herself for journey through time, key
Voyage over mountain through sky: no delay.
Floating candle glows in sad hour, bee
Of black flower breaks ultimate silence.
Time, mighty warrior, exerts savage power
In quietness. Unthwartable force—no sense—
Lifts her body, wafts mother that was, flower
Of welcoming, somewhere far away. Death,
Mysterious loss, impresses heart, glimmers
With pain, shines like grey pearl. Final breath,
Fragrant, numbers with life every hair, lures
Like shining angel as I weep devil's tear:
Inarticulate love wipes clean all fear.

Visitation

Bearing white candle, she rises like bold phoenix
From ash, whispers softly in cold darkness,
Smiling all the while, grins through fix
Of old tears. To earth she comes, far less
Alive than determined, like a witch, to leave word.
My mother, haunted by tender vision, extends
Her sleeves, folded twice with care, then a third
Time. Heart laced with pain—recently tended
By child's hand—she fills my open palm
With ray from sun, light from another world.
Eyes glinting like the lion, she turns—calm,
Silent—ascends as if forlorn: whirls,
Disappears. Solemn, still, she remains
Distant as sea, shucking cold earthen chains.

Riddles of the Tomb

Voice from bare earth cries into light,
Chants eternal wisdom, poses riddle
Of the tomb. Asleep in sudden night,
Woman hums ancient tune, strums fiddle
Of silence, closing chord of quietness.
Mother of still heart awaking never
Dictates supernal poem to timid guest
In darkness: waiting, invisible. Clever
Fingers of soil tend lifeless body,
Caress aged skin still smooth—gentle
Sage, seer in blind grave. Dame flees
Toil of time, burden of day. Gull
Of lustral love magically wings her
To region of pearl, teases legends that were

Bright June

Elysium, angel-wings know more
Than I, bereaved: dead to eye, to hand
At waking hour, gone from touch, door
To living. Mother of common blood, in land
Of poetry, you wear gown of pearl,
Await bridegroom, prince of peace. Mistress
Of time, concubine, I weep, girl
Of isolation, unwed. In orphan dress
Tattered with love, adorned with patches of care,
I surrender to absent arms, wishes rent.
Aged in a day, dully weary and bare,
I pray for flowers of noon: stylus bends
In dark night to fashion pictures of you
And me as we were, we two, in bright June.

Jewel

The other side, irresistible,
Teases behind the wall, wildly forges
One final truth, invincible.
Glory of the sunflower gorges
Daylight in garden of remembrance:
Death struck irrefutable, majestic,
Smote clean the neck and tongue, kindly lanced
Boil of life (pure and sharp), sick
With ease. Time took her fee: golden witch
Shrieked like bald eagle at midnight. Mother
Responded, broken child of hours, rich
With living. Gilded moments lie in treasure,
Buried beneath grass forever now:
Heart-coin of sorrow, red jewel, I bestow.

Evening Serenade

Mute flowers of heart charm new bride
Of lasting grave. Leaves of love rustle in
Sheer light, shine like flames ablaze, abide
Though life is still. Face to face, she wins
A vision as we darkly look through glass.
Hour of painful birth is past: the time
For death has come, for lying beneath the grass.
Mother—flutesong, magic poet's rhyme,
Evening serenade—gestures now
In silent tomb. Shimmerings of laughter fade:
Eye glimmers no more. On wide water prow
Sails toward final rest, in bright shade,
Blessed long ago. Morning and night she sought
Wine of love: on crystal door she knocks.

FATHER

Old King

Gravedigger tolls the bell for my life
In him: bats whistle cannily for his soul.
Gloom descends on royal bed, sharp strife
Invades peaceful home of long ago.
From glorious chair, high, but empty now
Of golden words, old king, once triumphant,
Descends. Father shakes with fear, bows low,
Counting seconds until end. A chant
Of mercy, prayer of lasting hope begins
Journey without end, holiday
Without song, grim game: no one wins.
Spell stills kisses for father: like cartoon, I play
Before feet without sound. A mummy, I hear
Marching, glimpse bleak coffin—cold, near.

Nothing

Hand of father, stranger alive now dead,
Broke phoenix in two, teenage child
Moaning low, maimed in darkness: shreds
Of innocence—fledgling bird gone wild.
Quasi-loving touch, forever bound,
Beat to earth, down, after jingling
Silver coins on Judas' scandal ground.
Crowd praises beloved man turned to nothing:
Ashes in urn quietly bury crime.
Heart—mish-mashed: hands feverishly sew
Torn pieces, pull needle, forcing rhyme.
Now at funeral, formal show
Preserves silence, ever-muted tongue.
In effigy he dwells: reluctantly hung.

Glass of Time

Old bones ache with impotence, drown
In glass of time: mighty sands
Mark the hour, lose themselves, sound
With quiet dream. Tiny fingers ban
Breathing, children's touch swiftly closes
Music box of age. Nails unclipped
Bite his old flesh—grow, gash, doze
Long minutes. Sighs shuffle, muscles dip
Away; father stumbles, falls, wipes
Familiar tears, wisely offers gold
For care, dreading family grimace, gripe.
Last hours lie heavy on his lonely soul,
Hang unwished for in empty room
Filled with echoes of the sweeping womb.

GOD: THE CRUCIFIED

Dead Lamb Walking

Simon strolled blithely to Jerusalem,
Eyes ablaze with wondrous sight: dead
Man walking. Simon stupidly looked at them—
Wardens mocking, piercing obedient head,
Lashing back—compelled, somberly took
Cross from dying man who walked before,
Victim like any other, yet primal look
Of sorrow in his eyes. Simon bore
Thick cross of Jesus for a time, key
To mystery, urn of pain. At first
Cyrenian relieved the Jew—but He
Alone bore eternal shame. To be cursed
By God and man for sins not His—the time had come,
Lamb before swift shearers marching dumb.

Scarecrow

I hang in loyal love, crow-plucked eyes
Open in dark night. Wind rustles straw
Or rags, whistles ragged heart. New flies,
Old faults, now purged, eat trustingly raw
Flesh, drink blood. I shooed black crows away
Beyond pale sky, hanging through cold dew—
Brightly stiff with purpose, unafraid.
A battered thing I seem, though a few
Know why I died: I killed birds old and new.
I shunned the winged ones with my bare hands,
Hole-sore wrists, now dry. That hour they flew
Away, metamorphosed, to alien land
Invincible, infernal. In long love
I hang, glad king, gentle as the dove.

Red Leaves

Three men walk together in bright day:
Determined, speechless, anxious—ascend green hill.
Figure lies down on wood, knowing he may
And may not stir as two hammers fill
Each palm with blows of nail, stab both feet
Like pigs, then raise tree between odd thieves:
A violent, a sordid hour in heat
Of sun on hill of green amid red leaves
Of anguish. Son hangs pure in sky—left
To sins of world. In magnanimous heart,
He searches for one rock His father cleft:
Alone he suffers, pierced by pointed dart,
Arrow of abandon. Shut from earth,
Son in desolation loses hope, all mirth.

Dr. Katherine Brueck holds a Ph. D. in Comparative Literature (English, French, Russian) from the University of Illinois. She is Professor and Chair of the English Department at Mount Saint Mary's University in Los Angeles. Dr. Brueck has contributed scholarly articles to journals in a variety of humanistic disciplines. She authored *The Redemption of Tragedy* (SUNY Press 1995) in which she develops a theory of Christian tragedy based upon Simone Weil's mystical Christian Platonism. She has spoken on Simone Weil at colleges and universities throughout the United States and in England.

More recently Katherine has contributed sonnets to literary journals including *Blue Unicorn, The Lyric,* and *Troubadour.* She has given poetry readings in Tri-City Michigan with the Rustbelt Roethke Creative writers group and also more locally in Southern California. She is currently working on a book of imaginative short shorts devoted to the theme of adult relationships with children.

Katherine is indebted for her present work *Voiceless Love* to the editors at Finishing Line Press in Georgetown, Kentucky; to the poets at Rustbelt Roethke Creative Writers Retreat in Tri-City Michigan, two of whom, Katherine Fishburn and Patricia Harkin-Pierre, continue to offer poetic inspiration and have become close friends; and to her husband Don Brueck who has voluntarily acted as manager throughout the publication process.

www.ingramcontent.com/pod-product-compliance
Lightning Source LLC
LaVergne TN
LVHW091233080426
835509LV00009B/1262